The Freedom of Lavenders

AUGUST REYNOLDS

The Freedom of Lavenders

AUGUST REYNOLDS

atmosphere press

to my family

Table of Contents

Foreword

As a rule of thumb, I stick mainly to Irish poets. Of course, there's Robert Frost, for whom I've carved out an eternal exception to this rule. But, after all, it's only because Frost is the closest thing to Seamus Heaney that we can produce in America. It's not that I've intentionally made a habit of closing myself off to other authors — no, in fact, I've always been certain that real artistic and intellectual growth comes only from keeping oneself open to new voices — but it remains true that Heaney and Yeats and Joyce are able to capture something almost lyrical about the human condition.

I've chosen for myself a life of public service, whether in political office or in the practice of law. This regrettable predilection for the boring naturally makes one a student of history, and with Irish *bona fides* to boot, I feel at home in oft-repeating a quotation from Senator Moynihan:

"There's no point in being Irish if you don't know the world is going to break your heart."

There are as many French, English, and Portuguese Reynolds' as there are Irish Reynolds', but I've chosen to trust August Reynolds, the author of this collection and one of my oldest friends, when he tells me that his red hair is not genetic coincidence, but rather an evidentiary component of his prowess as an author, further corroborated by a fully-developed understanding of what so many young people today have discovered as their human condition.

Unlike Tynan-Hinkson or Kavanagh, Reynolds is writing in an era when people everywhere, particularly people of the youngest generations, are getting a taste of the heartbreak that the world has to offer. That's why I'm particularly grateful for this, the first collection of his poetry. Having no artistic talents of my own, I'm in no position to offer a poetic exegesis, no position to offer homiletic analysis. I am, however, well-positioned to find the unabashed melancholia of this work to be an apt reflection of what this world occasionally proffers.

Reynolds introduces himself to the literary world through this collection as what David Foster Wallace would call a rebel. Whereas the rebels of old would risk the gasp, that is to say shock or outrage, the rebels of today face different risks. The risk of appearing earnest or awkward, or the risk of being greeted with rolled eyes and accusations of sentimentality or melodrama, is what is wagered in Reynolds' un-ironized sentimentality.

Rich with accessibly authentic emotion, the works herein are wholly modern in their approach. Simple. Fragmented. Part of a tapestry that is as spalled as it is diaphanous. Gleaming with emotionality and limerence for a girl unnamed, or perhaps just a Caulfield-esque concern for innocence.

In the galactic scope of Reynolds' work, we find the syzygies of hopefulness and lugubriousness, of innocence and loss. We escape the internal brabble of insecurity and find the quintessence of a new, youthful authorial direction in a modern poetic landscape. And best of all: he's part Irish.

- Liam J. Watson

EPITHET CALLED SHITSHOW

these
words
are
not
an
art,

they
are
an
escape.

treat
them
as
such.

i
don't
mean
to
trap
you
here,

nor
do
i
mean
to
send
you
hiking
up
in
heels,

but
there
is
something
endearing
about
that,

isn't
there?

The Freedom of Lavenders

her lips were numb.

i could tell.

"ah, so this is brilliance, aye?"

smiling, she turned.

a plead, i suppose,
making it to the
wood.

"you should let them wilt this time, Honey."

i think she finally did.

Limn

let's hold each other

until the metal
fencing decays
at our feet

until the grass
learns our feet
are home and
browns under us

us

let the trees wilt,
Honey,

let the trees wilt.

Low-Flyers

will i die without
reaching paradise?

would i ever get tired
of it?

despite my best
efforts, i find
that even the
most powerful birds
find cages to reside
in

and the train
still passes on its
tight schedule

tick tock
tick tock
tick tock

rot in hell;

the devil laughs
at us all

and more.

American Dream

the devil made it
living under
my skin

staring at the mirror
devoid of —

man?

and smoke poured
from my parted lips

hitting the ceiling

and covering
later what
remained of —

me?

as it fell, grounded
on level fields, finally,
locked with all we left
behind

together.

See

december,

that is when i
believe it all
started

anyhow,
anyhow,
anyhow,
anyhow,
anyhow,
anyhow,
anyhow,

with you,
the words never
seem to come

i mean, sometimes
i think of leaving
you, but does that
make me a
bad person?

i've done your
work,

i have.

earlier,
when i asked
for your help,

may i ask,

why were you
slow to stand?

i'm sure she'll see this

but i don't know when

chasing our Freedoms in

the west,
west,
west,

the pioneered west
of youthful bliss

foraging in the
cool mud;

i miss it.

but we've aged, i get it.

slightly, now, dethroned.

but, before we part again,

here:

i pressed a petal for you.

The Freedom of Lavenders II

this machine has fallen
many times before
and i find it hard to
write sometimes and sometimes
i even pray

i pray

but i couldn't tell
you why, ever.

this hike is growing,
ascending horribly at a
speed i cannot
track

and i swore to the
blue that the trees would
die, but i haven't seen that

i haven't.

oh, tell me, love,
how can we pursue
that Freedom when
our flowers shrink
in the windowsill
by our own damn neglect?

Iron Reserves

i sit at the top
of that concrete
monstrosity

"call me August now, okay?"
i say

many shared smiles
were had here

i place a dead flower
where i sit

it was so beautiful

oh how it was just that

beautiful.

Nolan's County

15 minutes was all
she said she'd give

sitting, knees up,
staring at the
canopy

her canopy

chopping the very
air she sits in, hitting
any and all

as she feels that
wonderful beat
pulsate through her
like a hurricane;

like he made her
his. back when.

she always could
feel that.

really, i guess
i just want the world
to melt away and
turn to dust

reduce to nothing

whilst we sit there
blue bench
barefoot

in that tarnished
green patch with you

by the grounded
stars

again.

the happenings

four orange slices
float atop my borrowed
glass

and my small speaker plays

and the dog yawls

and the neighbors stare

and there are lights
hanging from the tin

— a broken man
in the easiest of ways

shattered glass

bat

golden hands

that field…

planting your feet
and swinging
so great that
you spun
with it

and, as you realized
your victory,

your destruction,

turned, and walked away.

your hands could've pollinated
the earth then but even she
can't have you.

For Edna

tell me,
how will this
grand story of
ours end?

will the piano
standing on a
solitary leg
fall, finally?

will the sea-battered
ships rust and sink
this day's rising
tide?

will the wine
drop from her
soft mouth,
ruining the white
blouse?

or will we stand more?

suffer more?

declare at last…

tell me, please,
that it was pretty,
right?

the white, i mean.

Wong

i travelled the
park we used to
brave when we
chased fireflies
those many years
ago

didn't stay very long

i couldn't

the memories
still ripe and vivid
and alive and kicking

in this
now lost place

as the people went by

by by by

this twisted twisting;

this spiraling

—

man is still a dog

this damned twisting
is most unpredictable
when unleashed

but when fed and pet,
content.

when?

when did we settle?

all just a fairytale

i wish i had
a million beautiful
lies to give to
you

but all i have are
these truths and
this fading machine

i love you
or
at least i
think i do

but to brave
the sea,

you must first
acknowledge its
depths

fuck its
creatures

and steal
the king's
crown

i love you
or
at least i
think i do

i love you
i love you
i love.

The Freedom of Lavenders III

we were in the
woods

not long

i imagine

before we couldn't
stay any longer…

how i wish we
could've combat
the world,

found a home
amongst the

quiet

but, now, i fear
it wouldn't work
as we hoped
back then.

oh, your blue eyes

oh, the way it all
seemed

but you're gone
and there is
nothing i can do
about that now

now…

please,

i hope i see you
again soon

i'll be there,

waiting,

black suit and all

flowers in hand.

Headstone on Fifth

c'mon, c'mon!

it's raining
VERY hard
outside and
there is this
HUGE puddle!

        her boots were
        purple and they were
        tall

c'mon, c'mon, hurry UP!

i think the water
will be up to my
ankles this time!

Lye

the moon fell in
my bedroom window
upon a bottle of lye

now in motion
ascending up to
the lips on a man to die

from the lips of
man to die or me
jumping with the moon's goodbye

love it all now
and hold on with might
through the kiss of the moon's lye

///

i couldn't begin
to describe why
i am at odds with
myself

as if my mind
would fit better
in another's body

dostoyevsky was
right, i reckon:

it is always easier
to convince your
mind of a wrongdoing,

acknowledging an
enemy as weak,
wrong, and faulted

it is hardwired

even when that
is yourself.

the mirror spats
back at me

and all i'm missing
now is the hatchet.

Home, Kin

green on gray
with sharp-edged
windows and desolate
archways, stands
the type of place
you'd encounter
a dragon;

eyes yellow and
sinful with bands
of the new youth

drunk

in a phalanx

ready to defend.

let it come

and for her,

that song.

the gravity and weight of it all

we scream at the
heavens just to
fall, now,
on a spiked
earth

and, maybe now,
you can break me, too.

honestly

well, listen —

i'm tired of
chasing a love
that you
effortlessly
call healthy

i want to
chase that
crippling light,

i want those
plants to wilt,

i want immortality
with you,

you.

but i can't anymore

i just can't.

can't so long as
we parade around
calling this
double-edged sword

not.

The Freedom of Lavenders IV

the woods,
the woods…

oh, how the wood
is silent;

how i wish my
mind was so.

The Last Look

i'm not ready

"..."

i've been trying
to write this
for months now,

to tell,

to get it on a page,

and, well,

i guess i'm
not ready either.

Try

i tried writing
about the boy
on the bus —

novels can be
written about one
hour of a broken
man's life.

i tried,

but to produce
this, i sell
my organs to the
birds and give
power to that court
which holds too
much already…

what am i to do?

what am i to do?

Metal and Grated Stairs

the walls
up here
are high
enough to
stop a
car but
sometimes i
like to
wonder if
they could
stop me
just me

falling to
stop all
the monotony

falling to
free me
from my
pervasive thoughts

falling to
revive the
dandelions below

but then
i shake
my head,
yes, and
snub the
cigarette my
mouth held
and slowly
move back.

On Solitude

creases every few inches,
the curtains drape
down
and down
and

D
O
W
N

begging to be opened
begging to move
begging me to
let the light in
but i enjoy the
black the surrounds me
and the dense quiet,

i really do,

the world will not like this
twirling mess of limbs
and pain and guarding
apathy;

i feel its hand on my
shoulder and breath on
my neck and i see its smile
in the corner accepting what
lives in it:

nothing.

let me remain as nothing.

Break

he chased them
all that night,

the flickering, fallen
stars.

so gentle.

i remember when he
told me, others

beat him with belts

choked him with hoses

still, i see all
the scars

the starved body

split lips

black eyes

missing hair

bruises

—

broken in all
but spirit,

he gently caught
seven that night.

Sour Milk

the damn trees

there, not bothering
a soul

following the
road's edge

how i wish i
could see
them again.

—

lea

oh, the Freedom
was lost in foul
mud.

rain fogs my glasses

walking through
blood-soaked fields.

i remember

we danced and danced
until our sides hurt

until we couldn't
distinguish between
rain or sweat;

we wanted sweets
and metal and
warmth and —

well,

just for a second,

i thought we actually
found it.

filling the back pages

my last effort
to save a life
began after
he let me
come back to
visit that day
after following
the red and
i guess i always
knew it would
happen

that i would,
really, this
time

but the walls
up here are high,
it's different

nothing like what
they wrote about

but i always
forget that,
i mean,
it isn't my
first time
seeing it all

have i mentioned
that yet?

oh, and i forgot to
say goodbye

and you'll tell
them this time, too,

won't you?

he was there, once,

staring out at the
wood

the bleak, gray
wood

and sometimes
i like to wonder
what happened
to the

boy

on the bus

living through it all

all those years ago…

it's a funny thing, really,
hearing of him run

and run.

but he is again;

he is.

South-Bound-Bend

cell a6

jail

prison?

well, the story
is quite lousy:

he was driving down
route 11, saturday,

and i don't know
what was running
through his head
in that moment,
well, well,
anyhow,

he wrapped his car
around a tree just past
the bend at the bottom
of the state

and i swear it took
months for him to
recover fully and,
when he did, i swear it,

really,

they ushered him
to the house with
no delay —

how warped it is,
this society,
that a man cannot die
on his own terms
and time

without punishment.

Listen Carefully

"i want
something —
someone —
to believe in
again, that's all,
you know?"

i ask

"yes."

she says

"do you really?"

i ask

"well, i just
think that you're
cynical."

she says

my drum beats too loud
it is out of tune
it is broken
it beats too differently

— you fucking failure —

i've caged them and the
crows now speak on my
behalf.

"you really think that?"

i ask

"yes."

she says.

the no names

winter trees
don't cling to
their leaves.

you, too, must
know when to
let go.

the plead

by tomorrow's morning
light, will you
find me?

i won't ask
you to,

not directly,
at least.

please, oh, god, please

find me
find me
find me

this wood…

oh, i fear
i cannot survive
one more frigid night

and my soul wrings
in the very mud i
lie in once more.

Journey

i long to
walk on stone
that lay
dormant for
centuries

built by
my ancestors

with wind blowing

rain falling

at last,
with a full heart.

Acknowledgements

"Iron Reserves" also known as "When We Walked" at the time of publication, was first published by *The Red Cedar Review* in 2021 for their 2020 journal.

"he was there, once,", "Break", "i'm sure she'll see this", and "Metal and Grated Stairs" though written slightly different at the time of publication, were first published by *Origami Poems Project*.

About Atmosphere Press

Atmosphere Press is an independent, full-service publisher for excellent books in all genres and for all audiences. Learn more about what we do at atmospherepress.com.

We encourage you to check out some of Atmosphere's latest releases, which are available at Amazon.com and via order from your local bookstore:

Reflections in the Time of Trumpius Maximus, poetry by Mark Fishbein

Drifters, poetry by Stuart Silverman

As a Patient Thinks about the Desert, poetry by Rick Anthony

Winter Solstice, poetry by Diana Howard

Songs of Snow and Silence, poetry by Jen Emery

INHABITANT, poetry by Charles Crittenden

Godless Grace, poetry by Michael Terence O'Brien

March of the Mindless, poetry by Thomas Walrod

In the Village That Is Not Burning Down, poetry by Travis Nathan Brown

Mud Ajar, poetry by Hiram Larew

To Let Myself Go, poetry by Kimberly Olivera Lainez

I Am Not Young And I Will Die With This Car In My Garage, poetry by Blake Rong

Saints of Sacred Madness, poetry by Joyce Kessel

About the Author

August Reynolds has had many poems accepted for publication in places such as *The Red Cedar Review, Philologia, Origami Poems Project,* and more!

Hailing from Blacksburg, VA, August was once an English Literature student at Virginia Tech, but decided to fully pursue his love for writing outside of the academic scope. He currently resides in a quaint place by the river consuming food that is probably too bad for him whilst he writes.

You can check him out online on Instagram @d.try9!